TOMORROW

TOMORROW

A Memoir of Love, Family, and Dealing with Dementia

Andrew J. Rickert

ARCHWAY
PUBLISHING

Archway Publishing books may be ordered
through booksellers or by contacting:

Archway Publishing
1663 Liberty Drive
Bloomington, IN 47403
www.archwaypublishing.com
1 (888) 242-5904

Because of the dynamic nature of the Internet, any web
addresses or links contained in this book may have changed
since publication and may no longer be valid. The views
expressed in this work are solely those of the author and do
not necessarily reflect the views of the publisher, and the
publisher hereby disclaims any responsibility for them.

Any people depicted in stock imagery provided
by Thinkstock are models, and such images are
being used for illustrative purposes only.
Certain stock imagery © Thinkstock.

ISBN: 978-1-4808-3374-6 (sc)
ISBN: 978-1-4808-3375-3 (e)

Library of Congress Control Number: 2016910887

Print information available on the last page.

Archway Publishing rev. date: 7/7/2016

CONTENTS

AUTHOR'S NOTE

The purpose of this book is to share a true experience with a loved one who is suffering from dementia. There are many different avenues and circumstances one experiences during the course of this disease. This book offers only one set of circumstances that have been experienced, starting with initial suspicion of a loved one's abnormal behavior through the actual diagnosis and aftermath. The main focus is on the physical, medical, spiritual, legal, financial, and administrative aspects as the Power of Attorney (POA) for the loved one suffering from dementia disease. There is an emotional side of this story, which is why I wrote this book.

Dementia is a disease that is going to expand to many more people in the next forty years. The American Academy of Neurology estimates that 4.7 million people with dementia in the United States in 2010 will increase to 13.8 million by 2050. The annual estimated cost for dementia ranges from $157 billion to $215 billion. These figures provide a general idea of the magnitude both in volume and in resources.

The objective is to provide the actual conditions that existed with this loved one and how these conditions were addressed. These are the true and actual events that have been experienced. The individual names and organizations are real in order to preserve the integrity of this factual document. Hopefully, this will help others in dealing with similar situations.

Most of us go through life not thinking of ever being faced with sometimes an unbearable situation like dementia of a loved one. Once faced with this condition, as next of kin you are presented with medical, spiritual, financial, legal, and humane situations that make you wonder how in the world this happened. Based upon your love for this person, you unknowingly will be able to withstand all of the hardships and disappointments that are presented to you.

This is a story of a person who is loved by all, had a great career as a secretary, and was a breast cancer survivor. She is my sister Edna. Edna lost her husband, Les, to diabetes about four years earlier after a prolonged illness of this terrible disease. Les was a firefighter with the Saint Louis Fire Department. They were married for over forty years. They had no children. But Les had children from a previous marriage. They had a rather uneventful lifestyle during their marriage. They did a little traveling to visit my family and me in southern Maryland and to visit Les's children in Texas. Edna enjoyed gardening, taking care of the lawn, and visiting neighbors. While our parents were alive, Edna and Les would visit them frequently. Edna spent endless hours taking care of Les in the hospital and nursing home during his final years in addition to working forty hours a week at a bank.

Edna retired shortly after Les's death in 2011. After her retirement, Edna made frequent visits to Jefferson Barracks Cemetery to visit her husband's grave. This was done three or four times a week. This may seem a little excessive to some, but the grieving process differs among people. I could appreciate Edna's feelings, which was an expression of her love for Les. This was probably amplified by the fact that she never had children of her own, and Les was her one and only true love.

Edna was a very neat person. She was always well dressed and neatly groomed. Her house was always clean and neat as a pin. My wife, Bessie, stayed overnight with her and Les when I was on travel for the federal government. Bessie was amazed at how clean and neat everything was, even with the dog. But that all changed shortly after my brother-in-law's death.

Edna loved her computer and browsing the Internet and communicating through e-mails. We exchanged e-mails two and three times a week.

But all of a sudden, the e-mails stopped because the computer stopped working. This was difficult for me to understand when the cost of computer repairs, or the cost of a new one, was so low.

Edna also loved dogs. She had a dog most of the years she was married. The dogs also loved Edna. She would take them for walks, which provided a plus for her physical health and the dogs. Her dogs were always clean and well groomed. You will see later on in the book how this changed and presented a clue that something was wrong. Maybe we did not want to believe something was wrong.

Edna also was a victim of elderly prey by a culprit doing handyman work to the known amount of $50,000.

Edna's coworkers thought the world of her and had nothing but good things to say about her. This also applies to her neighbors, friends, and relatives.

Chapter 1
BACKGROUND

The Rickert family consisted of our mother and father, my sister Edna, my younger sister Mary, a half sister Nettie, and me, the only boy. We were raised on a farm near Renault, Illinois, except for Nettie, who was older than us and for the most part lived in Winchester, Illinois. Our parents were married in Winchester, Illinois. They were very poor and hardworking, trying to recuperate from the Great Depression. The farm we were raised on was owned by a Saint Louis realtor. We all had to work hard caring for the chickens, turkeys, hogs, cows, and crops. We were a very religious Catholic family. Our mother converted to Catholicism a few years after their wedding and became the most devout Catholic in our family.

I recall walking to grade school in 1946 with Edna. I was ten years old, and Edna was eleven. This was on a gravel road one mile and a half long to Renault. Our grade schooling was in one room with all eight grades and one teacher. These walks to and from school were memorable days. We would talk about the day's events, good and bad. We went to a Catholic high school, Saints Peter and Paul in Waterloo, Illinois, which was eighteen miles from where we lived. Saints Peter and Paul High School later became Gibault High School, as it is now known. We caught the school bus in Renault after walking a mile and a half and did the reverse on the way home, regardless of weather. Fortunately, we had sufficient clothing, even though most were hand-me-downs. The roads to Waterloo at that time were either gravel or blacktop most of the way, which caused the bus to be much slower.

Edna was very smart compared to me. She willingly performed her share of the chores on the farm. She had a cat named Lucky because of her three colors white, yellow, and gray. I was about as ornery as a brother could be to his sister and would tease her about Lucky getting lost. She took very good care of Lucky. This is probably why she thought so much of dogs later in life. Edna learned how to play the piano and played the organ in the Renault Catholic Church, Our Lady of Good Council parish during her high school years. I enjoyed listening to Edna play the organ while serving Mass.

Edna earned the honor of May Queen in her senior year at age seventeen. This was a very formal ceremony held in the Saints Peter and Paul Catholic

Church in Waterloo. Edna was very neatly dressed as if she were going to the prom. I was so proud of her being selected for this honor, which was great. It saddens me to think of what eventually was in store for Edna. At the time, the future seemed full of endless possibilities.

Shortly after graduating from high school, Edna went to work at the Burkhart Manufacturing Company in Saint Louis, Missouri, as a secretary. She would come home on weekends by bus to Waterloo, and we would arrange to pick her up there and drop her off on Sunday evening for her return to Saint Louis.

Edna married Lester Jenkins, as mentioned earlier, in 1975. They bought a home in Saint Louis at 5216 Robert Avenue. Les was a fireman in the Saint Louis Fire Department. Edna and Les never traveled much and certainly did not have an extravagant lifestyle. Edna never drove a car for several years. When she did start driving, she would chauffer her neighbor Rose and a few elderly ladies in the neighborhood to Saint Rafael's Catholic Church on Sundays. After Mass, they would often go to breakfast, normally at the local Steak and Shake.

I, Andrew (Andy) J. Rickert, was not as smart as Edna, or maybe I was just lazy in school. I, too, worked hard on the farm. I never liked to milk cows, so in the spring when we were putting in the crops, I would con my dad into letting me drive the tractor, plowing, in the evening and he would milk the cows.

I would plow until eight or nine o'clock in the evening and then get ready for school the next day, which also required me to be out of bed by 5:00 a.m. to help with the chores prior to school.

I served Mass from the fifth grade on. On weekdays while in grade school, I would serve 7:00 a.m. Mass and then go to school starting at 8:00 a.m. There were only four people in my class, including me.

Money was very scarce, so when I could pick up some work, I jumped at it. I removed the ashes from the church coal furnace, cut the cemetery grass, was water boy for the thrashing crew, helped the neighbors put up hay, and looked forward to serving Mass at weddings and funerals, where I would normally receive a dollar or two gratuity. That was a lot of money in those days of 1948 through 1954.

Shortly after graduating from high school, I joined the Marine Corps, where I served for three years and three months from June 1954 to September 1957. Fortunately, I didn't have to face combat. However, the military training was a definite asset in my future decision for a career and in particular facing dementia of a loved one and my own battle with cancer.

Shortly after completing my enlistment in the Marine Corps, I met my wife, Bessie, and we were married shortly afterward. I worked for defense contractors and then for the Federal Civil Service where I retired. Then I went back to work with defense contractors, and now I am permanently retired.

In the early years of our marriage, I had an opportunity to work as a technical writer on the Titan I Inter-Continental Ballistic Missile (ICBM) system in Denver, Colorado. I never had much money, so I borrowed $100 from Edna to make the move. Can you imagine that in today's world? Moving from Belleville, Illinois, to Denver, Colorado, with a wife and two small children on such few dollars was unbelievable if not stupid. But we made it safely and successfully, even though we had to sacrifice. Bessie and I have four daughters, nine grandchildren, and six great-grandchildren.

Based upon my career in Federal service, I accepted a promotion to move to the Army Material Command in Alexandria, Virginia. We were living in southern Maryland when I retired from there. At that time, our two oldest daughters were married and we had five grandchildren. This is the reason we decided to stay in southern Maryland. Trying to get Bessie to move away from her grandchildren would have been next to impossible.

My youngest sister, Mary, followed the same path as Edna and me for school. She also was very intelligent and is liked by all. Mary also followed the same music path as Edna and played the organ in Renault for Our Lady of Good Council parish. Mary was married to Norman Melliere shortly after high school and is the mother of five boys. They bought a home in Prairie Du Rocher, Illinois, shortly after their wedding. In addition to playing the organ for Saint Joseph's parish in Prairie Du Rocher, Mary also taught music to children and worked at the school in Prairie Du Rocher, where she retired in 2015. Norman suffered with diabetes and cancer the last six years of his life and passed away in 2014. Mary continued to play the organ at Saint Joseph's parish after she retired. Like Edna, she didn't drive until recent years. Now she drives the car to local towns, but is reluctant to drive in larger cities like Saint Louis.

Nettie was the oldest child in our family. As such, I don't remember much of her early years. She lived with us for a short time in Renault while attending the public high school in Waterloo, Illinois. Nettie spent most of her time after high school with our aunt Irene (Mom's sister) in Winchester, Illinois. While in Winchester, Nettie married Jim Roosa. Jim worked in law enforcement and accepted employment as a railroad detective, which required them to relocate to Green River, Wyoming. They had three boys. Nettie worked for Union Pacific Railroad as a stenographer and retired as such. Jim passed away a few years ago, and Nettie passed away just recently in 2014.

Kim Scott (officially Michael Kim Scott) is our second cousin. Our aunt Irene's daughter, Patricia, is the mother of Kim. Kim stayed in touch with us primarily with Edna and Mary throughout the years. Patricia passed away at an early age. As a result, our aunt Irene, Kim's grandmother, raised him. Kim is a very likeable person. He worked as a law enforcement officer in the city of Winchester. Later, he worked for the State of Illinois Civil Service in Springfield, Illinois, where he retired. Kim also is a devout Catholic and was ordained as a deacon at Saint Mark's Catholic Church in Winchester. Kim is working very hard as a deacon due to the shortage of priests in the Catholic Church. Kim not only serves at Saint Mark's parish in Winchester but also the satellite parish in Pittsfield, Illinois.

In summary of our family background, it should be noted that Edna really only has three close living blood relatives: our sister, Mary, second cousin, Kim, and me.

Chapter 2

OBSERVATIONS

Throughout the years, Edna and I would exchange e-mails two or three times a week. She would enjoy surfing the Internet and relaying to me sights she thought would interest me. This went on for many years. Then about five years ago, in 2010, the e-mails stopped. This was shortly after Les's death. Edna explained to me that her computer had stopped working. I suggested that she get one of these computer whizzes to fix it or perhaps get a new one since hers was rather old. I knew it wasn't money that was holding her back. I felt certain that she had sufficient funds. Regardless, I would have been more than happy to buy her a new computer. I even suggested that I ask Mike, my son-in-law, to visit her and take care of the computer problem since he is an IT specialist. But she refused. I felt that Les's death may have been the reason she was acting this way. This went on for a few years, which caused us to use the telephone to communicate a couple of times a week, in addition to visiting a couple of times a year.

Normally when Bessie and I would return to southern Illinois to visit relatives, we would arrange to visit Mary and Edna. This would either be at a restaurant where Edna and Mary would meet us or Edna would join us at Sunday Mass at Saint Joseph's Church in Prairie Du Rocher, where Mary played the organ. After Mass, we would meet at a local restaurant for breakfast. When Mary's husband, Norman, was in the nursing home, we would drive to Red Bud, Illinois, to visit him. I remember at one of these gatherings Norman told Edna that she should replace her old computer. Edna was rather upset with Norman's comment. However, she let it slide for Mary's sake. I certainly agreed with Norman, but I was smart enough not to say anything.

It was very difficult for Bessie and me to understand why Edna, who loved her computer so much, would not either fix it or replace it. Edna certainly didn't look like she was suffering from any illness. She acted as she always did. So we just let it slide and didn't pursue it any further. This was our first observation and where we went wrong. We should have pursued it by perhaps visiting her at her home and correcting the computer problem. This visit may have identified other conditions in Edna's behavior that would have caused us to pursue remedial action. I certainly regret not pursuing this observation.

Our second observation was altogether different. A few years earlier, Bessie and I flew to Salt Lake City, Utah, and then drove to Green River, Wyoming, to visit my sister Nettie. This was a very enjoyable trip, as Nettie was in good health and her three boys were most hospitable. I had asked Edna and Mary to join us, but they refused. I could understand this because both Edna's and Mary's husbands were in ill health at that time. Later, as Nettie was getting up in years and in a nursing home, I was prompted to make another visit to Nettie. At this point, both Edna's and Mary's husbands had passed away, so I was a little more forceful this time in inviting them to join Bessie and me. I volunteered to pay all the expenses, which I did. Mary had never flown before, so this presented another potential problem. However, she agreed to join us, probably because of her boy's insistence. I made all of the arrangements with the airline, rental car, and hotel. Edna promised to provide a suitcase for Mary to use since she didn't travel much and didn't have one. In phone calls to Edna prior to the trip, I would remind her about the suitcase for Mary. She would tell me that she had forgotten and would do it tomorrow, which was unlike Edna. Since Mary never drove in Saint Louis, I agreed to pick her up in Prairie Du Rocher, and we would go to Edna's house, park the car, and take a cab to the Saint Louis airport. The return flight wasn't scheduled to arrive in Saint Louis until midnight, so we agreed to take a cab back to

Edna's house, stay there the rest of the night, proceed to take Mary home the next day, and Bessie and I would continue visiting relatives.

The part of the plan where we would stay at Edna's house didn't work out. Everything was working well on our departure to Wyoming, where we picked up Mary, who used a handbag to carry her belongings since Edna had forgotten the luggage, and got to Edna's house that morning. Edna hadn't packed anything until that morning. When we arrived, I had to use the bathroom. In entering her house, there was a strong odor of dog urine, a small amount of dog feces on the floor, and a light out in the bathroom. I really didn't know what to do. I was literally shocked, but I didn't want to say anything and embarrass Edna. But I also knew that we couldn't stay there when we returned. So we proceeded on with our trip. During the trip, Bessie and I decided to use the excuse that we had to be at Bessie's sister Wilma's house in Sparta, Illinois, early in the morning after our return, and after we picked up the car at Edna's house, we would drop Mary off at her house and then spend the rest of the night at Wilma's. Also during the trip, Edna never brought her blood pressure medicine. This bothered me, but she didn't seem concerned at all. Bessie and I closely watched Edna for signs of high blood pressure, which fortunately didn't occur.

Our trip was very successful in terms of scheduling, flights, rental car, and hotel accommodations. Nettie's boys were glad to see us and treated us very well. Nettie, now ninety-one years old and in the nursing home, seemed to remember us as best as we could tell on the first day, but again not sure. We visited her the three days that we were there. The second and third days of our visit assured us that she wasn't recognizing us. The following week after our return, Nettie passed away. We were so fortunate that we got to see her one last time before her death.

Our experience with Edna on the Wyoming trip was the second observation that should have been taken more seriously. Hindsight tells me that we should have gone back to Edna's house after the trip to Wyoming to see in more detail the problem from the odor in her house and the dog feces on the floor and to find out what could be done. But we didn't do this and returned home to Maryland. Again, I regret that we didn't follow through.

A year after the Wyoming trip, I retired for the second time. This was very fortunate for me to have time to address personal matters. A year and a half after retiring, I got another surprise in trying to call Edna. Up to this point, I was able to call her a couple of times a week with no suspicion of a problem. Then I heard the phone company say, "The number you have called has been temporarily disconnected." Normally this means that the bill hasn't been paid. Edna always paid her bills on time. Wishful thinking on my part was that it was some kind of technical glitch. So I tried calling three days in a row, receiving the same result. Now I really started worrying. I thought the best thing to do at this point was to contact some Saint Louis agencies that deal with aging. I was a little embarrassed to call the police because I had to contact them a couple of times earlier when her phone was off the hook and I didn't want them to think that I was a troublemaker. However, I would have if I had been unsuccessful with calling the Saint Louis agencies on aging.

I tried calling different places without success. Finally, a person said that I needed to call the hotline based upon what I had told him, which I did. The state representative supervisor for the State of Missouri Department of Health and Senior Services answered the phone. After explaining the situation to him, he told me that he would go over right away to see what was going on and get back to me as soon as he could. He called back that afternoon to tell me that Edna looked good physically, but her house was in disarray. There was dog feces all over the floor, the odor was atrocious, papers were scattered all around and piled up on tables, including unpaid bills and uncashed checks, and the refrigerator was well stocked with food, some of which had expired. There were mice running around, and the dogs were hostile, but Edna was able to quiet them down. The larger dog, Willie, had an open sore and appeared in dire need of medical help. The man had told Edna that her brother, Andy, was worrying about her. She responded, "Andy is a worrywart."

The state representative supervisor didn't pull any punches and laid it on the line. The house needed massive straightening up. If it was not done soon, the city would condemn it. The Saint Louis Health Department was so advised, and if not promptly corrected, the house would be condemned. The humane society was notified of Willie's condition, and if Willie wasn't taken to a veterinarian soon, the animal control people would remove him. Edna needed psychiatric help, and if she didn't obtain it on her own, the state would take over, and a ninety-hour psychiatric review would be conducted. If the review showed that Edna should not live alone, the state would put her in a home and her assets would be taken over by the state. The sheriff would be contacted if she resisted the psychiatric review or going to a home. He told me that Edna was well-to-do. How he found this out without our knowing and so fast was beyond me. The state representative supervisor assigned Edna's case to one of his assistants in his office. I felt a little relieved knowing that Edna was all right physically. But her living conditions left me embarrassed, saddened, and upset.

All of this occurred shortly before Thanksgiving in 2014. I told the state representative supervisor that I would be there soon to assess the corrective action that was needed and pursue whatever was needed to be done in accordance with his findings if he could hold off bringing the state in. He made it clear that I needed to get there soon, and agreed to hold off until I was able to get there, providing I moved quickly.

This was the straw that broke the camel's back, and the third observation on Edna's mental health deterioration. All of these observations, starting with the computer problem, the various problems observed on the Wyoming trip, and the problems noted by the state representative supervisor were telling me that we needed to quickly pursue corrective action. Bessie and I got our things together as quickly as we could for the drive to Saint Louis, which is nine hundred miles from our home in Maryland. We would have flown, but being eighty miles from Thurgood Marshall Airport in Baltimore, the hassle of handling luggage on and off shuttles and requiring a rental car in Saint Louis, it was much simpler to drive even though it took longer. We had to reschedule some doctor appointments and make sure we had sufficient medicines to last. Bessie was very supportive of what needed to be done. Without her support, I may not have had the strength to address Edna's situation. Needless to say, our Thanksgiving dinner in 2014 was less enjoyable than in previous years.

Chapter 3

FIRST VISIT
11/29/14–12/8/14

Bessie and I left for Saint Louis early the morning of November 29. This is a two-day trip now that we are in our senior years. I have driven from our home in Maryland straight through to Saint Louis in my younger years. We stayed overnight in Mount Sterling, Kentucky, and proceeded on the next day to Collinsville, Illinois, where we would stay for the duration of this trip. The reason we stayed in Collinsville instead of Saint Louis was because of the Ferguson, Missouri, rioting and the Comfort Inn in Collinsville gave us a reasonable rate for our room. Collinsville is less than twenty miles from Edna's house in Saint Louis. The motel accommodations were great. However, there was icing conditions predicted for the next day, which was a major concern. We had a nine o'clock appointment the next day with the state representative supervisor and thought it would be wise to find out where his office was located. So before we retired that evening, we tried to locate it. Thank goodness we had a global positioning system (GPS) in our car. We located his office without too much trouble.

The next morning there was ice, and traffic on the main thoroughfares was proceeding slowly. We really didn't know how treacherous the roads were, but knowing the importance of proceeding, we decided to go. Fortunately, we made it. When we arrived at the office, we were greeted by the assistant assigned to Edna's case. The entrance to the reception area was crowded with people waiting for appointments and hearings. We were escorted to the supervisor's office. The office was a typical government office. We were introduced to the supervisor, who appeared very concerned about Edna. He reiterated the same concerns he had earlier told me over the phone. They showed us pictures they had taken earlier, which was very depressing. He told me that I had best get a power of attorney (POA) for Edna and possibly guardianship. This was necessary in order to keep the state from taking over and bypassing Mary, Kim, and me. I could tell that the supervisor was speaking from experience, and I took his advice very seriously. Cases liked Edna's could wind up in the courts, which could be a lengthy and costly process. He provided us with a phone number of a government legal service organization that could prepare a POA at no cost and provide any further legal advice that may be needed. I really got the impression that the supervisor was trying to help us. Also, his assistant provided us with a list of companies that do cleanup work. The supervisor said that they would be by Edna's house later in the week to see how we were doing and that I should keep his assistant informed about the status.

We then drove to Edna's house. I knew what to expect, but I wasn't sure that I had the strength to face it. Bessie said that I had her full support and together we would get through it. Edna greeted us with open arms. She appeared to be in good physical shape, but the house was in disarray, as the supervisor had explained. The dogs raised a ruckus, but Edna quieted them down. Normally, Edna would only have one dog, Willie, but she inherited Cutie, a small Jack Russell from her sister-in-law who had recently passed away. The odor was so bad that Bessie had to wear a mask. Fortunately, Bessie had the instinct to bring masks. Additionally, there were dishes piled up in the kitchen sink along with eggshells on the floor. The pantry, refrigerator, and freezer was packed full of food and most of it had expired. This was a real sign of hoarding. Nothing had been done to straighten things up from the supervisor's earlier visit. There was an occasional mouse running across the floor. There were numerous bottles of various alcohol products on her buffet. One would think that Edna was an alcoholic with all of this booze. Edna never had the appearance and actions of an alcoholic, so I figured these were items left from her late husband. Edna could carry on a conversation so normal that you couldn't tell that anything was wrong until she started repeating herself. She kept remarking about my hairline receding and that I looked like our late grandpa. Then a few moments later, she would say that I looked like our late dad. She seemed so happy that Bessie and I were there to visit. She did not suspect that we were there for other concerns affecting her health.

Edna's neighbor Rose stopped by to see what was going on. Rose stayed on top of everything going on in the neighborhood, which was good from our point of view. Others may have referred to her as a busybody, but we sure didn't. She was real good to Edna and a great help to us by having a key to Edna's house and looking after things when Edna was away. I asked Rose about the alcohol, and she said the only alcohol she had seen Edna consume was an occasional can of beer when sitting on the front porch in the summer evenings. This sounded reasonable to us.

I told Edna that we had to get this mess straightened up because she couldn't go on living like that. Edna said she would take care of it tomorrow. She became rather defensive and said that I was there to visit and not to work. This conversation went on and on. I kept reminding her of what the state representative supervisor said about the state taking over. That didn't bother her one bit. Also, Edna hadn't had her hair washed or cut for some time. Her fingernails needed manicuring, and her hygiene was very, very poor. I offered to take her to the beauty shop, but she adamantly refused. Bessie offered to wash her hair, but she refused, saying we could do it tomorrow.

After much discussion, Edna said she wondered who had turned her in, meaning that she thought someone from the neighborhood reported her situation to the State of Missouri. Bessie told her that I had reported my concern about her welfare to the state representative supervisor when I couldn't reach her by phone. This prompted the supervisor's visit, who then reported back to me about her situation, which prompted our visit. You would have thought Edna would express some displeasure with me, but she didn't. I was fearful that Edna would cease to speak to me and order us out of her house, but she didn't. Maybe she didn't believe Bessie or didn't want to believe her. She started talking about something else. I don't think she believed that I was the one responsible.

I was getting nowhere with Edna. So I thought that maybe our cousin Kim could help. I called him and explained the situation to him. He said he would be at Edna's house on Wednesday. He said that he had a funeral to conduct on Tuesday and would otherwise be there immediately. Edna always had good things to say about Kim and was very impressed with his judgement. I asked Kim to wear his deacon Roman collar in hopes that would get Edna to cooperate. This was the last approach I could think of to get things moving outside of getting the state involved, which I would have as a last resort to preserve Edna's health.

During our discussions, a handyman, who had known Edna from earlier work he had done for her, stopped by and introduced himself. I told him the circumstances we were faced with and that I was getting ready to call some companies that the state representative supervisor's assistant had provided me earlier to get the cleanup process started. The handyman said he and his cohorts could do this job. I thought that it might be best to have someone Edna knew do the work as opposed to a company we knew nothing about. Therefore, we asked the handyman to give us a price. He said that he could do the job for $600 in cash. The handyman then wanted to talk to me in private, so we stepped out on the front porch. The handyman said that Edna owed him $200 for work he had done on the garage. He didn't want to bother her and upset her. So I said we would increase his bid to straighten up the house to $800. He seemed delighted with my response. However, Edna still refused to let the work begin. So I got the handyman's phone number and told him I would call him probably by Wednesday with the decision to proceed.

We then decided to go to lunch at the local Steak and Shake. I was going to drive even though Edna was still actively driving at age seventy-nine. Bessie slipped on the ice going down the front steps to the driveway. I about had a heart attack in fear that Bessie had broken any bones. Fortunately, she was fine. Everybody working at the Steak and Shake seemed to know Edna. To me this meant that she frequented the place, which gave me concerns about her regular diet.

Edna told us that she would visit her late husband Les's grave three or four times a week. Les had been dead for four years. We all understand the grieving process that occurs when you lose a loved one. But three or four times a week after a death occurring four years earlier seemed a little excessive. Les was buried at Jefferson Barracks Cemetery in Saint Louis, which was only about ten miles from Edna's house. Perhaps being that close was why Edna went so often. Also, the grieving process varies by individual.

Since the straightening up the house was sort of on hold pending Kim's visit, I started the conversation on finances, the POA, and will. In an attempt to find the POA and will that Edna said she had, I went through several stacks of papers and her safe in the basement. We couldn't find the POA or will. The only other source I could think of would be the Saint Louis city courthouse. So we agreed to drive to the courthouse the next day and check it out. As a precaution, I called the legal services number that the state representative supervisor had provided to get the process started for a POA and will in the event we were unsuccessful at the courthouse. I was told that it would be a couple of weeks before we could get an appointment. So I put this action on hold, pending our success at the courthouse. Also, I wanted to discuss this with the state representative supervisor before spending money for a private attorney.

The remainder of our first day with Edna was spent discussing finances. This was not a simple task. We found out that Edna had a revocable trust at the bank she retired from, along with checking and savings accounts at the bank and two other banks, stocks with Textron, life insurance with Prudential, and who knew what else. When Edna retired from the bank, she was influenced by the bank to set up a revocable trust to protect her assets. Only the successor trustee and the trust principal could access the accounts in the trust. There were no documents showing the value of these accounts or the totality of accounts in the trust. There was one document as part of the trust showing a value of several hundred thousand dollars. There was nothing showing the accounts that made up the total trust, which started to bother me. On the income side, Edna was receiving social security and retirements from the bank, Textron, and the Saint Louis Fireman's Retirement from Les's service on the Saint Louis Fire Department. We drove to Edna's local bank to try to get a better handle on the accounts and values. We were able to get a copy of the revocable trust, but that was all. We could not get any information on the accounts making up the trust because I was not the successor trustee. Kim was. I asked Edna why she made Kim the successor trustee, and she said it was because he lived closer than I did and he was very trustworthy. She also said that she would rather have me as the successor trustee. The bank representative also told us that we would need an attorney to prepare a document changing the successor to me. Until that was done, I would not be able to obtain any details on the revocable trust for Edna. All of these loose ends were starting to affect me emotionally, but I knew I had to stay on top of things to protect her interests.

I needed to know if Edna had made her funeral arrangements. She said she had at the Ziegenhein Funeral Home, which was located only a few blocks from where she lived. She said that everything was paid for in advance and that there would an hour or so visitation in the morning and then move to the cemetery at Jefferson Barracks next to her husband's grave for a graveside memorial service. I said Edna don't you want to have a funeral Mass? She said no, which really bothered me. I know we are to abide by the wishes of the deceased, but being Catholic all her life, I thought that she would definitely want a funeral Mass. I thought it best to discuss this later with Kim since he was a deacon and may have some ideas on how best to approach this situation.

The next day, Tuesday, started with a trip to the courthouse, which was downtown and difficult to find parking. I drove with Edna giving directions, even though we had GPS. This was quite a chore with all of the walking and my chronic obstructive pulmonary disease (COPD). We were able find out that there was an outdated POA from her late husband, Les, assigning Edna as his attorney-in-fact for their assets. There was no will. So we were back to ground zero in terms of these important documents.

I called the state representative supervisor and his assistant to give them an update. I told them that the legal people he had recommended required us to wait about two weeks for an appointment. The supervisor told me that I needed to get a private lawyer because we couldn't wait that long on the government legal services. He recommended an attorney who dealt primarily in legal matters of the aging. He didn't seem overly pleased with the progress. Therefore, he said that he and his colleagues would be by Edna's house to see what was going on the next day, which was Wednesday. I then called the attorney to discuss the POA and will for Edna. Their paralegal answered the phone, and I gave her the details of Edna's situation. I was then introduced to the attorney, and I provided some further details on the requirement for Edna's POA. We made an appointment for Wednesday afternoon to complete the POA for both finances and health, making me the attorney-in-fact.

The next item I thought was appropriate was Edna's health. Her doctor had recently retired and as replaced by a younger doctor who Edna had visited only once. The prescriptions Edna was taking was for blood pressure and cholesterol. After our experience on the Wyoming trip, I wasn't confident that Edna was taking them regularly. I felt it necessary to visit the doctor's office with Edna and sign the HIPA form in order to have access to Edna's medical records in the future, which we did. Edna was agreeable for me to sign the HIPA document.

Now Wednesday was here with the visit of Kim and the state representative supervisor and his colleagues. It really was show-and-tell time to get things moving on straightening up the house. Kim arrived with his deacon Roman collar on, as I requested. We went through the normal pleasantries. Then the supervisor, his assistant, and the environmental health officer from the Saint Louis Health Department arrived. There was a person from the humane society outside, waiting to take the dogs, if needed. However, that didn't happen. The supervisor gave his normal stern pitch on what had to be done and the consequences if they weren't. This had little impact on Edna. The environmental health officer sat next to Edna and was very compassionate in trying to get her to agree to have the house straightened up. I was impressed with her tact. Then Kim sat next to Edna with his arm around her, talking very calmly about what she should do. All the time Edna was staring at his Roman collar. Finally, she agreed. At this point, we were happy to start seeing progress. I feel confident that Kim's presence saved the day. I told the supervisor that we had made arrangements to have the handyman do the work. He seemed more assured that we were making some progress. You would have thought that Edna would be upset with the supervisor because of his sternness, but to my surprise, she wasn't. She had nothing but good things to say about him. This was probably because he knew his business and left the impression that he was trying to help. His assistant was also a great help in assisting us with the details in fulfilling the requirements of the state.

I called the handyman to get started straightening up the house. He came right over with his crew and started work. They hauled a few truckloads of trash, outdated magazines, etc. to the dump. Edna was a typical hoarder. While this was going on, we kept our appointment with the attorney for the POA for both finances and health. Also, we had the attorney prepare another document stating that the POA superseded any and all previous POA documents. This was accomplished. Edna signed the POA documents in front of witnesses and wrote a check to the attorney for $1,100 for these legal services. The original copy of the POA was given to Edna. Later, Bessie told me that I should have kept the original for fear of Edna losing it. Also, I reminded the attorney that we needed a will prepared, but it wasn't a priority at this point. She said that she wanted to visit Edna first, which she did the following week. This was necessary in order for her to fully understand what we were faced with.

I received a call from the handyman later that evening at the motel saying that the health department representative stopped by Edna's house and was pleased with what was done. But before they would give approval, the basement had to be straightened up and an exterminator had to be contacted to get rid of the mice. The basement was really a mess with all of the things that Edna had hoarded over the years. I was happy with the health department review of the main floor but concerned with the basement requirement, knowing that this was going to be a monumental chore.

The next morning, Edna paid the handyman $800 in cash. The main level of the house looked much better. The handyman gave us a price of $1,500 cash to straighten up the basement and haul several loads of trash away. Edna agreed, based upon my recommendation. The handyman and his crew went right to work. We contacted Terminex for a one-year contract to get rid of the mice. We then drove Edna to the bank to get $1,500 in cash. I asked the teller how much Edna had in the checking account. She told me $91,000. I about fell on my face. I really didn't understand the wisdom of having that much money in a low-interest account. At least I knew we had money to work with. I didn't want to question Edna on why she had such a large amount in her checking account because I didn't want to upset her now that we were starting to see progress.

The handyman's daughter, who was in school at Washington University, stopped by Edna's house to perform some general housework for a little spending money. She dusted the living room furniture and figurines, which was a big job with all of the figurines Edna had accumulated over the years, and dusted the dining room furniture. Edna paid her twenty dollars. We asked her if she could stop by once a week or so and do housecleaning and to let us know if things were disorderly. She said she could, and Edna reluctantly agreed.

While waiting for the handyman and his crew to complete his work, we tried to persuade Edna to pay her telephone bill and reactivate the phone. She kept insisting that she paid the telephone bill. But contact with AT&T indicated that she owed over $300. This was probably four or five months without payment. We finally were able to convince her to use her credit card, pay the bill, and reactivate the phone. We now had a means of communication with Edna once we got home, at least for a little while.

When the handyman's work was finished, Edna paid him, and Bessie and I were thinking of returning home to Maryland. I contacted the state representative supervisor and his assistant and gave them an update on our plan for remedial action. He seemed appreciative of our plan and said he would continue to follow-up. We cautioned Edna to be sure to let the dogs outside to do their business. The odor was still very strong. If she didn't leave them outside, the house would soon be in the same disarray as before. I also asked Edna to straighten up the loose papers, pay the bills, and deposit the checks. She said she would tomorrow. I also asked Edna several times to put her utility and telephone bills on automatic payment at the bank. She adamantly refused. You would think that with her working at the bank for so many years she would have jumped at the opportunity for automatic payment. Evidently, Edna experienced some problems with automatic bill paying while working at the bank. She thanked us for helping her and hugged us as we were leaving. With that, Bessie and I left for home.

There were many things to do regarding Edna's health, finances, and general way of life. I had to stay in close contact with all concerned. I requested our attorney to start the process of preparing a will for Edna. I also asked her to look into changing Edna's revocable trust to have me as the successor trustee, replacing Kim. Kim was also in favor of this. I kept the state representative supervisor and his assistant informed as we proceeded. I figured as long as he knew that we were making progress with Edna, he would not have the state take over.

After a couple of weeks at home, I called the handyman to see if his daughter was by Edna's house to do some cleaning. He said that she tried, but Edna refused to let her in the first time. She then made an appointment to stop by again. In doing so, Edna wasn't at home. I called Edna about this and was told that she didn't need any help. I knew this was wrong but could do nothing about it being nine hundred miles away.

I received a call from the state representative supervisor's assistant, asking if I knew anything about MAPS. I said no and asked what that stood for. She didn't know and went on to say that she had received a call from a representative of MAPS. She said that it was some kind of program that deals with memory loss for the aging and suggested that I give them a call, which I agreed to do.

I called the representative, who explained MAPS (Memory and Aging Project Satellite), a program from Washington University in Saint Louis that has a grant from the National Institute of Health (NIH) to assist in the memory loss problem. She was interested in Edna's situation. She was also a registered nurse (RN). I gave her a rundown on Edna. She wanted my permission to visit Edna, which I gave her. I then called Edna to let her know about the MAPS representative's forthcoming visit. I had forewarned the MAPS representative of what she may expect on her visit with Edna.

The MAPS representative called me after her visit. She said Edna welcomed her. The dogs were very hostile, but Edna was able to quiet them down. She said there were dog feces on the floor, and the odor was terrible. Papers were scattered around, and there were mice. All this disarray had occurred within only a few weeks after Bessie and I had left. The MAPS representative said that Edna's hygiene was very bad and needed improvement. She gave her a brief memory exam and said she has signs of memory loss, which could be the early stages of dementia. She also noticed all of the alcohol bottles on the buffet and wondered if Edna was suffering from alcoholism. I told her that I had the same concern and passed on what Rose had told me about Edna only having an occasional beer while sitting on the front porch in the summer evenings. I told her that I thought the alcohol bottles were from her late husband. I told the representative that I would be scheduling another meeting with all concerned parties to include her.

The MAPS representative report was really not a shocker to me. With everything we had been through thus far, and with the dogs staying in the house, I wasn't surprised but rather saddened. I had appointments with a lung surgeon and oncologist in Baltimore (eighty miles from where we live) in early January 2015. These appointments were because of a Hodgkin's lymphoma I had been diagnosed with about four years earlier, before Les's death, and was now in remission. I have been on the six-month follow-up routine. During one of these follow-ups, a spot was located on my upper left lung that was thought to be from my many years of smoking. This resulted in my meeting with a lung surgeon in addition to the oncologist on these follow-up visits for monitoring. I not only had to concern myself with Edna's problems but also my own cancer condition. I couldn't delay these appointments, so I scheduled the meeting with Edna for January 12. I invited the MAPS representative, the state representative supervisor and his assistant, Kim, and our sister Mary after giving each of them an update on where we stood on Edna's situation. I made the motel reservations at the Comfort Inn in Collinsville, Illinois.

Chapter 4

SECOND VISIT
1/8/15–1/16/15

Bessie and I left home early the morning of January 8 for my doctors' appointments in Baltimore. Our plan was to leave Baltimore that afternoon after my appointments for Saint Louis. My appointments went pretty much on schedule. The lung surgeon noticed a small growth on the spot on my left lung. He didn't think it was malignant but thought we needed to discuss it further when I returned from Saint Louis. He said that scars don't grow, but it could be from a cold causing the growth. This really got my attention. I not only had to deal with Edna's situation but also my own possibility of continued cancer. We left Baltimore to take the northern route to Saint Louis, Interstate 70. If we were leaving from home, we would have taken the southern route, Interstate 64. As I drove west on I-70, I kept hearing the doctor's voice in my head over and over again. I kept wondering what I would do if the cancer had really returned.

We stayed near Washington, Pennsylvania, that night and left for Saint Louis early the next morning. It was subzero weather. We arrived at the Comfort Inn in Collinsville that evening. We were getting to be regular guests at the Comfort Inn, and they welcomed us with open arms. We decided to visit relatives over the weekend and hold off until Monday to visit Edna.

We arrived at Edna's house the morning of January 12. Edna was glad to see us, and the dogs went through their normal ruckus with Edna quieting them down. The house was still in disarray as earlier explained by the MAPS representative. I kept saying to Edna that this couldn't continue, and she would reply that she would take care of it tomorrow. All of the invitees showed up for the meeting. All except Mary had seen Edna's house earlier, so they weren't surprised. Even though I had told Mary how bad it was, she, her son, Troy, and his wife, Stacey, who drove Mary to Edna's house, were shocked. They all knew Edna as a very neat and well-groomed person, and it was very difficult to see her this way. I could see the sadness on their faces.

The state representative supervisor and his assistant, the environmental health officer, and the MAPS representative arrived shortly afterward, and we again went through the normal pleasantries.

Everyone in attendance realized that this was not going to be an easy meeting. You could readily tell this by their demeanor. I felt that we had legal matters under control as best as we could at that point.

The state representative supervisor gave his stern speech, which most of us had heard before. When he got to the part that he was going to take Edna for a psychiatric exam, Edna said that she was going nowhere. The supervisor emphasized that the sheriff would see to it that Edna would go. This must have gotten Edna's attention because of the expression on her face. Maybe the supervisor was finally getting Edna's attention. The MAPS representative said that the house needed a detailed cleaning and that Edna definitely needed psychiatric help. She said that the carpet needed to be removed because of the odor. Edna wouldn't have any part of that, even though there wasn't much choice. The MAPS representative said that she would see how soon she could get Edna into Saint Louis University Hospital for the psychiatric exams. I said that we would arrange for the detail cleaning. I also mentioned that I was trying to get Edna's utility and phone bills on automatic payment from the bank and that she refused. The state representative supervisor quietly asked to see my POA. After doing so, he told me to go ahead and do it because Edna wouldn't know the difference. I could tell by his demeanor that he had been through situations like this before. He also told me to get guardianship. I think the reason for this was to keep the state from taking over without court action against me as POA. The supervisor and his assistant were doing their best to help us.

The meeting was very helpful, and then we adjourned. We had a lot of work to do. I got in contact with the handyman to give us a bid on detail cleaning. He said he could do it for $1,300 with payment by check. This sounded a little strange because he always wanted cash before. So be it, as this made it easier for us in that we didn't have to run to the bank for cash. He would have his crew do an in-depth shampooing of the rugs and have his two cleaning ladies do the necessary cleaning and straightening up. When finished and accepted by us, we were to make the check out to one of his cleaning ladies. He said they would start the next morning and stay until the job was complete, no later than one day. This sounded reasonable to us.

We were in close contact with the MAPS representative, trying to get an appointment for Edna's exam. She said we needed to have Edna's medical records sent to the office that was going to do the exams. The next day, after getting the handyman's cleaning crew started, we took Edna to Hodap's restaurant for a chicken lunch. This was Edna's favorite restaurant. After lunch, we went to Edna's doctor's office to get her medical records faxed to the place the MAPS representative said to send them.

Edna provided directions in great detail, which made me wonder if she really had a mental illness. The next item was guardianship. I called the attorney's office later that day to get things started.

I needed to get the successor trustee on Edna's revocable trust changed to me. The local bank official had told me that I would need to have an attorney draw up the documentation to do so. I contacted the attorney's office to get the process started and faxed them a copy of the revocable trust. Also, I asked for the status of the will, and nothing had been done. I again told the attorney that the will wasn't a high priority, but I would appreciate it if she would keep it on her "to do" list.

The attorney contacted me the next day, saying that she couldn't do anything for me on guardianship because she was representing Edna and it would be a conflict of interest to also represent me. She recommended that I contact another law firm, which she recommended, who also dealt in legal matters for the aging. Also, she told me that she located a copy of Edna's will at the bank and that I should stop by her office and pick up a copy. This was good news and one less worry to deal with.

I called the recommended law firm and talked to the paralegal. I explained the details regarding Edna and that I needed guardianship and a document requesting the changing of the successor trustee on Edna's revocable trust to me instead of our cousin

Kim. The attorney called me later that day, saying she would represent me and that I would need to sign a retainer agreement and provide a $3,000 deposit. I agreed to do this and told her that she should draw up the agreement and mail it to me because we were planning to leave for home the next day. At this point, I had spent over $6,000 of our money in travel expenses and miscellaneous expenses. She also said that she was going to stop by and visit Edna. She wanted to see Edna's condition for herself because she needed this assessment in order to develop the proper plan for guardianship. I then told Edna of the attorney's planned visit.

Bessie and I knew that Edna's living arrangements were going to have to change. We suggested several alternatives, such as living with us in Maryland. We told her that her nieces and nephews would be so happy to have her near them and would definitely see that she received excellent care. She refused. Next, we asked her if she would consider living with Mary. Definitely she would not. Then we suggested that she could sell her house in Saint Louis and buy another in Prairie Du Rocher, where Mary and her boys could look after her and she could keep her dogs. Again, she would not. We also asked if we could arrange for someone to visit her daily to help with the house, manage her medications and personal hygiene, and see that she had a healthy diet. Definitely there was no need for that was her response.

The handyman and his crew finished their work, and the house looked much better. Edna wrote out a check to one of the cleaning ladies for $1,300. Edna never kept a check register like most people do. Instead, she relied on the carbon copies, which was really a haphazard way to manage a checking account, and she didn't pay much attention to that method either. I again asked Edna to try to keep the dogs out of the house to do their business. She said that the dogs were her family and she would treat them accordingly. However, she did say that she would try. I in a way could understand Edna's feelings toward her dogs. She didn't have any children and very few relatives. I called the state representative supervisor and his assistant and gave them an update of our accomplishments and plan for the future. They seemed reasonably pleased. With that, Bessie and I left for home in Maryland.

While at home, we stayed in contact with all concerned parties. The MAPS representative was having difficulty getting an appointment for Edna at the Saint Louis University Hospital in the near future. She was also going to pursue Barnes Jewish Hospital. She was doing an excellent job in trying to help us with Edna's situation. If you have never been through something like this, there are so many details that need to be considered.

The attorney called me a week or so later and said guardianship was a very serious matter. She thought that the state representative supervisor was oversimplifying it. The attorney visited Edna a few days earlier to see for herself Edna's condition. She also was concerned that my POA was done recently and that in the eyes of the court it would look very suspicious, like I was trying to move in on Edna's assets. She therefore recommended that we not pursue guardianship at this time. Perhaps after we got the psychiatric exam and knew more about Edna's mental condition we could visit guardianship again. I agreed with her recommendation.

I started the chore of getting Edna's bills paid automatically from the bank as the state representative supervisor had suggested. Even though he said that she wouldn't know the difference, I still felt a little guilty in that I was doing something on Edna's behalf without her knowing it. This turned out to be more difficult than I thought. The phone company, AT&T, was easy. I was able to handle everything over the phone. Laclede Gas, Ameren Electric, Metropolitan Sewer District, and the Saint Louis City Water District were more difficult. They all required a copy of my POA before they would do anything. Some of them also required a copy of my driver's license, date of birth, and social security number. So I forwarded my POA and additional information to them, and we finally got it taken care of. All that I was trying to do was to make sure they were paid in a timely manner. You would think that they would have jumped at this without any red tape.

Knowing the situation with Edna's memory, I thought that I had best contact the Ziegenhein Funeral Home to verify what Edna had told me regarding her funeral arrangements. They verified everything Edna had told me. This was another worry that I did not need to address. But I still needed to see what we should do regarding a funeral Mass without going against her wishes.

I knew that Edna would eventually need some form of assisted living, whether it was in-home care or at a facility. I called a few organizations, such as A Place for Mom, and got a general idea of the types of care available and the cost. I also contacted the Cardinal Ritter Senior Services to see what was available. They had vacancies at an assisted living facility near Edna's house at a reasonable monthly rate. At this point, I was able to get a sense of Edna's finances and knew she could afford it. Edna would have her independence to come and go as she pleased, be fed three meals a day, and have her medications and hygiene monitored closely. Bessie and I again suggested that she also consider moving in with Mary in Prairie Du Rocher, or selling her house and buying one in Prairie Du Rocher. This way, Mary and her boys could look after Edna and make sure that she took her medications as prescribed and was eating properly. Another possibility was to have Edna move in with us in Maryland. This would have been the best alternative for Bessie and me because we would know how Edna was being cared for and our children would be more than happy to help. But Edna would have nothing to do with these recommendations. We decided to again present these thoughts to Edna at a future visit in a little more forceful manner.

Kim visited Edna a week or so after we returned home. He said that they had a nice visit and went to lunch at Hodap's. Kim sensed that Edna knew that something was wrong with her mind by her comments. Her poor hygiene again was very noticeable. The house was also starting to return to its deplorable condition.

I received a call from the state representative supervisor's assistant saying that she had received a call from a bank saying that they had received and cashed several checks signed by Edna to someone who was very suspicious. The checks started in October 2014 through January 2015. They were in increments ranging from $1,500 to $5,000 for a total of either $42,000 or $50,000. She would not tell me what bank or any further details except that the bank put a hold on any further checks to the suspicious person that were signed by Edna. She wanted to know if I knew anyone in Saint Louis with his first name. I said that the only one I knew was the handyman's. I told her that it couldn't be the handyman because he was too professional and nice. Anyway, I gave her his phone number. I also gave her an accounting of all the financial transactions I was aware of with the handyman. These were the $800 cash for the initial cleaning, the $1,500 cash for straightening up the basement and trash removal, and the $1,300 check for the detail cleaning.

This really got my attention. Something had to be done for Edna's psychiatric care real soon. I contacted all concerned parties and scheduled another visit. My goal this time was to get Edna into psychiatric exams and care as soon as I could. The MAPS representative was to get something set up at Barnes Jewish Hospital. I made motel reservations at the Comfort Inn in Collinsville, Illinois, for February 20 to February 27.

Chapter 5
THIRD VISIT
2/19/2015–2/28/2015

Bessie and I left home early Thursday morning, February 19. I was hoping that the MAPS representative would get an appointment at Barnes Jewish hospital while we were in transit, but we had difficulty communicating with her while traveling. We had nothing in terms of an appointment, prescription, contact point, or any other documentation normally required by a hospital for admittance. I was determined that we were going to do everything we could possibly do to admit Edna, regardless. I called Edna and told her what I was up to, not knowing if she would be willing or would rebel. She said okay. This sort of told me that she knew she needed help. She said she would try to get her neighbor Rose to watch the dogs. What a relief for Bessie and me. We stayed overnight in Mount Sterling, Kentucky, and proceeded the next day to Collinsville, Illinois. The Comfort Inn was again happy to see us.

The next morning, which was Saturday, we drove over to Edna's house. Even though Edna agreed over the phone to be admitted to the hospital, I still was apprehensive about her keeping her word. Edna again was happy to see us, the dogs raised their normal ruckus, and Edna was able to quiet them down. You would think by now that the dogs would have known us. Edna had not done anything about packing clothes and toiletries for her hospital stay. That really didn't surprise us because of our Wyoming trip experience. Edna had on an old pair of tennis shoes that she had worn working in the yard the previous summer. Her hygiene, hair, and fingernails had not improved. But for me that didn't matter. We were going to the hospital.

Edna gave us directions to Barnes Jewish Hospital even though we had GPS. She was very familiar with the city of Saint Louis after living there for sixty years, plus her late husband Les was at Barnes before he passed away. We arrived at the emergency room as the MAPS representative had instructed. We used the valet parking and proceeded in to the check-in counter, not knowing what to expect. I explained the situation with Edna at the counter, using the state representative supervisor's name and organization, and was then welcomed with open arms. What a relief.

After going through the administrative check-in, they said they currently didn't have a bed but would later that day. I told them fine. They also required a copy of my POA. They took us to another room to wait. Several doctors stopped by to talk and to examine Edna. One doctor called me aside because I was the POA and said that it appeared that Edna had dementia. That really didn't surprise me after all that we had been through. They even provided us lunch while we were waiting. I had never experienced this kind of treatment at a hospital.

The MAPS representative called while we were waiting and wondered how things were proceeding. When I told her that we had Edna admitted to Barnes Jewish Hospital, she couldn't believe it. She, too, thought we would have needed some authoritative documentation, or at least a point of contact. Whatever she had done to admit Edna to Barnes was now history. She said that she would visit us on Monday.

Late that afternoon they had a bed for Edna. After getting settled in, we opened some mail that we had picked up at Edna's house. Edna was getting to the point that she wasn't opening her mail. One of the letters was from the Southern Commercial Bank with a statement for January 2015. There were about ten canceled checks with all except one made out to the handyman. They ranged from $1,000 to $5,000. This was for only one month. There were other checks from October 2014 through December 2014 that we didn't have. This really upset me. I felt betrayed after supporting the handyman earlier to the state representative supervisor's assistant. I asked Edna what the handyman did to warrant these checks. She said that he had done a lot of work in the basement and had to get permits, etc. that was very costly. I said that I didn't see anything he had done that would justify that kind of money. She insisted that what he had done was well worth it. I suggested that we prosecute him, but she wouldn't have anything to do with that suggestion. I didn't want to pursue it further at this time because I was fearful it would not be advantageous to Edna's examination. But I was going to discuss this later with our attorney.

The nurse told us that the doctors would start their examinations the next day, which was Sunday, and that Edna would be involved most of the day with the examinations. With that, we told Edna that we wouldn't be by Sunday due to her examination activity and would visit relatives instead. We would see her Monday morning. Edna always asked Bessie how her family was and was pleased with our plan to visit them. With this, we said good-bye and then went to the motel.

Monday morning rolled around pretty fast. We went to the hospital right away, hoping that we would receive some form of diagnosis. This was wishful thinking. Edna told us that they did very little on Sunday. The hospital personnel told us they would be doing more that day. There were a couple of psychiatrists to see Edna, but there was nothing conclusive. Rose called several times, complaining about the dogs and the difficulty she was having feeding them. I told her to do the best she could and that I would be there as soon as I could. The MAPS representative stopped by and was trying to do the best she could to find out what was going on with the examination. She also contacted the social worker for status and provided us with little results. She said that we probably wouldn't know the results until Wednesday. The MAPS representative was very helpful in assisting us through this traumatic experience with Edna.

Tuesday went by without much happening. The psychiatrists stopped by again to talk to Edna. The nurse improved Edna's hygiene by washing her hair and bathing her. Rose called again, saying that the dogs were out of dog food. I told her that we would stop by the store and get some dog food and drop it off, if she could be there to open the door to Edna's house. Rose was the only one who had keys besides Edna. We got the dog food and proceeded to Edna's house. Rose was at the house and let us in. The dogs were very hostile. They were probably missing Edna. We finally were able to feed them and then returned to the motel for the evening.

On Wednesday, things started to happen. We were told that Edna definitely had dementia and could no longer live alone. I told them that I had located an assisted living facility near Edna's house. They told me that she could not live in assisted living and had to be admitted to a nursing home with a dementia ward. The social worker on Edna's case would locate a suitable nursing home. Later that day, the social worker said that she had located a nursing home that could accept dementia patients. Evidently, some nursing homes are not equipped for dementia patients. She told me that the nursing home was Mary, Queen and Mother Center at 7601 Watson Road, Saint Louis, Missouri 63119. She gave me the contact there, and I was to call them. This nursing home was part of Cardinal Ritter's Senior Services.

I called the nursing home and was told that they could accept Edna and started to explain the policy with Medicaid. I now had a little better idea of Edna's finances, which were around $1 million, not counting her house. It was hard to envision that a secretary and a firefighter could accumulate such wealth. But you must realize that they lived a rather simple life over those many years. Also, I served on the Board of Trustees earlier for the Charles County Nursing Home in Charles County Maryland, and I knew a little on how nursing homes operated. I told her that Edna would have to be private pay due to her financial status. She said it was $223 a day. I told her that I was Edna's POA and that we would be admitting her tomorrow. She said that would be fine and she would need a copy of my POA.

Bessie and I then told Edna that she could no longer live alone and asked if she would consider moving in with Mary. Edna said absolutely not. Edna really didn't appear shocked when we told her she could no longer live alone. I feel that she suspected that something had to be done. Then we suggested that she buy a house in Prairie Du Rocher so Mary and her boys could look after her. Again, she said absolutely not. Then we suggested that she move in with us in Maryland. We received another absolutely not. This was enough for Bessie and me to stew over that night and left for the motel. The MAPS representative called me that evening for the status. When I brought her up to date on what was happening, she recommended that we have an ambulance take Edna to the nursing home. Things happened so fast that I was apprehensive as to how Edna would react when I told her she had to be admitted to a nursing home. She had told me earlier that she would never go to a nursing home.

Thursday was going to be a very busy day. We not only had Edna's nursing home admittance to deal with, but also what were we going to do with the dogs? We had to get rid of them. We arrived at the hospital early and told Edna she had dementia and that we had to admit her to a nursing home. This was not an easy task, but Edna accepted it much better than I thought she would. I think she realized that something wasn't quite right with her mind. This again was another great relief. We made arrangements to have an ambulance take her to the nursing home. Bessie was busy on the phone contacting places that would take dogs. After several calls, she finally found a place that would take them. They would confine them for five days and then put them up for adoption. The cost was sixty dollars per dog. With all of these things happening with Edna, I never had time to worry about my potential cancer.

The ambulance came for Edna. They wheeled her out on a hospital bed, and she seemed content. We followed the ambulance to the nursing home. Upon arrival, they escorted us to a patient's room. The home seemed first class. There were no bad odors, and it was very clean. Many nursing homes are not this way. They showed her where her clothes closet was, etc. They counted the money she had with her, which was a little over $400. They then locked up her money and purse in a safe. Edna didn't have any additional clothes and shoes with her. So we contacted Mary and told her to try to get up to see Edna as soon as possible and asked if she could stop by her house and get some clothes and shoes. Bessie gave her a list of what Edna needed.

Then they took Bessie and me to the administrative office to sign papers and to provide a copy of my POA. While we were signing papers, they took Edna to the Hope ward, which is for dementia patients. On leaving the nursing home, we stopped by a nearby post office to do a change of address and have Edna's mail forwarded to the nursing home. Things were happening so fast that we did things automatically without much thought. We then left for the motel to think about caring for the dogs.

We now had to work out the details on how we were going to handle the dogs. We finally agreed that covering the backseat of my car with bedsheets from Edna's house would be the best and put the dogs there. Keep in mind the dogs hadn't been bathed in months. My car was a small Hyundai Elantra, so we figured on possibly two trips. Also, I needed to stop by the attorney's office to sign the retainer agreement and drop off the $3,000 check.

Now it was Friday with a snowstorm forecasted later that evening. We went to Edna's house to cover the backseat with bedsheets and to attempt hauling the dogs. We stopped by Rose's house to get the key. Willie was very hostile, so we chose to take Cutie and worry about Willie later. I carried Cutie to the car without incident. Cutie was excellent in the car for the entire ride to the animal control location. We thought we had to pay sixty dollars based upon what Bessie had been told the day before. But they told us that since we delivered the dog, we owed nothing. I felt like I had just won sixty dollars on the lottery. Our next big hurdle was Willie. We returned to Edna's house and tried to get him to the car without success. We tried everything we knew along with Rose's help. We decided not to pursue it any further that morning because we had an appointment with the paralegal to sign the retainer agreement and pay the fee.

The paralegal met us at their office and took several notes on the details of Edna's case and contact points. We mentioned the problem we were having with Willie and our desire to leave for home ahead of the forecasted snowstorm. She said that her sister had just finished school on handling dogs and needed some practice. She volunteered to contact her sister to see if she could help. Her sister said yes and agreed to meet us at Edna's house shortly after lunch. Bessie and I stopped for a quick lunch on our way back to Edna's house. Then we all met at Edna's house about the same time, including Rose. The good Lord must have been looking out for us because who would think you could get help with a hostile dog at a lawyer's office?

The paralegal and her sister tried to get Willie to let them close in order to attach a leash. They even used candy to coax him, but with no success. Rose went next door to the neighbor's house that was occupied by a policewoman. She came over and tried without success. We explained to her the difficulty we had in locating organizations that would take dogs. I then called the state representative supervisor to see if he could refer us to someone who could help, thinking that he had all the contacts. But he couldn't offer any help. He wanted to know what I was going to do to prosecute the handyman. I told him that I had more important things to do in getting home to deal with my cancer situation. I never heard anymore from state representative supervisor. The police lady then said she would make a few phone calls to some of her contacts. She made a connection with someone who told her if we could get a check for sixty dollars to a downtown address, he would make sure that someone would be there to pick up the dog later that evening. The paralegal, knowing that we needed to leave very soon in order to stay ahead of the forecasted snowstorm, told us that if we would give her the check for sixty dollars, she would take it to the downtown office and wait at Edna's house until Willie was picked up. What a relief. We did that and left for home.

Later that evening, the paralegal called us while we were on the road and said that Willie was picked up and walked very calmly into the trailer. Those people who handle dogs have the knowledge and equipment to deal with these situations. This was another relief for Bessie and me. It was hard to envision that you could get an attorney's office to help you move dogs. We made it home barely ahead of the snowstorm.

Now with Edna's house being vacated, there was no need for a telephone, so why should we pay the monthly bill for an unused service? It is normally a simple matter to discontinue service. But I had to go through a mountain of red tape to accomplish this because the phone was in Les's name.

We had a lot to do with getting things straightened out on Edna's behalf. But first I had to deal with my cancer situation. We made an appointment with the lung surgeon, Dr. Burrows, for consultation at the

University of Maryland Hospital Center in Baltimore. Dr. Burrows spent over an hour with us, explaining the pros and cons of radiation verses surgery verses doing nothing. He said he would present my case to a group of his peers, radiologists, and lung surgeons and get their recommendations. I am sure a biopsy was considered. But in my case, the spot on my lung was so small that removal was in order. He explained the extent of my surgery by comparing my lungs to two loaves of bread. Your right lung is larger than your left lung. Pretend that your right lung has twenty-five slices of bread and your left lung has twenty slices. He told me that when he got through with my surgery, my left lung would have seventeen slices. What a simple way to explain a complex situation. He could see that I was leaning toward surgery and emphasized that before he would do surgery, I would have to have some tests performed. Depending upon the results, he would determine if he could schedule surgery. These tests were pulmonary because of my COPD and treadmill stress tests. I completed the tests, and surgery was scheduled for March 25.

My daughter Kathy, who is a registered nurse, and her husband, Tim, drove Bessie and me to the University of Maryland Hospital Center in Baltimore. The surgery was successful even though the spot on my lung was malignant. I didn't know before the surgery that it was malignant. Dr. Burrows said not to worry because he had gotten all of it and no radiation or chemotherapy was required. This was good news. I was confined to the hospital for two weeks. This was because I had a little setback due to a medication that caused me to be delirious. All the time that I was in the hospital, I was thinking, if not worrying, about Edna. Bessie visited me every day and had tremendous courage that we would survive this ordeal.

Spring and summer were approaching faster than we would have liked. Something needed to be done to maintain Edna's yard and grass cutting. We discussed this with Rose, who recommended that the person, Joe, who cut her grass could also cut Edna's. We contacted Joe, who agreed to cut the grass when needed for twenty dollars a cutting and to bill us directly. Edna's lawn was very small. One would think that as POA I should have put the house on the market and avoid the costly maintenance. However, the house was part of the trust, and I was not the successor trustee and therefore had no authority to do so. Plus, there was a lot of work that had to be done to make the property marketable.

Kim and our attorney went to Edna's house to look for valuables that needed to be secured. They located some coins, jewelry, and documents from her safe, which were removed and placed in our attorney's safe. All items removed had to be documented on an inventory list. They located unpaid traffic tickets and court summons. These tickets dealt with going five miles per hour on an interstate highway, going the wrong way on a one-way street, and other citations. Edna was delinquent in appearing in court, which resulted in the court summons. Her driver's license was revoked. It is a wonder she didn't do harm to someone or herself by driving. Our attorney said that she would straighten things out with the city and county officials, which was a tremendous relief to me. Our attorney was able to obtain Kim's resignation as successor trustee on Edna's revocable trust. Kim, as likeable and trustworthy as he is, didn't want the responsibility. Our attorney now was in position to discuss placing me as the successor trustee with the bank.

It should be noted that the successor trustee is responsible for all management aspects and issues regarding the trust. Our attorney's discussions with the bank resulted in her recommendation to me to have the bank serve as successor trustee in place of me. The reasoning for this was that the bank would do this at a reduced fee since Edna was retired from the bank and they had the expertise to successfully manage all aspects of the trust. This would be difficult for me to properly execute living nine hundred miles away. The bank would then be responsible for selling the house and car, etc. I fully agreed with our attorney's recommendation. Prior to this, I couldn't get any information on Edna's revocable trust from the bank. Now I was informed about all aspects of the trust. In fact, I was inundated with papers and reports from not only the bank but also from all of the investment organizations used by the bank for Edna's assets. Our attorney transferred Edna's valuables and documentation from her safe to the bank safe. The 2014 income tax return that the paralegal was working on was also transferred to the bank. We earlier had our personal CPA apply for a six-month extension on Edna's behalf for submission of the 2014 tax return. The bank assigned a representative as the point of contact for Edna's revocable trust.

Edna seemed to be adjusting well to her new surroundings in the nursing home. I wrote her letters each week for about three weeks that she never read. I then decided to discontinue the letters. Bessie left stamps with her to write letters if she so desired. I don't think she ever used them. Edna was going on nursing home outings to dinners, plays, shopping, etc. and seemed to be happy.

Late one evening, we received a call from the nursing home saying that Edna was upset and a little hostile after returning from a nursing home outing. She started to pack her things and was going home. This was not the first occurrence. They were able to pacify her but wanted to discuss with me a remedial plan for preventing future occurrences. The next day, I called the nursing home and talked with the head nurse in the Hope wing. Evidently, there was some internal disagreement between the social worker and the head nurse on the best approach for resolving Edna's behavior. The head nurse proposed temporarily suspending Edna's outings and confining her to nursing home activities, which were plenty. This, along with the medication that the psychiatrist prescribed earlier that day, should help Edna. I agreed. Then I was asked to send them an e-mail to this effect. I agreed and did so. Hopefully, this would eliminate the squabble between the social worker and the Hope wing head nurse.

I was very concerned about telling Edna that we needed to sell her car because she could no longer drive and sell her house because she would no longer be living there. Also, I knew that Edna would want to know how her dogs were. My concerns with Edna in addition to trying to recuperate from my surgery were overwhelming. Finally, I figured that the only way to get relief was to contact the psychiatrist. Based upon a call I had received earlier from a psychiatric physician's assistant reporting on his visit with Edna that were positive, I called the psychiatrist. I explained the situation and my concern about upsetting Edna by telling her that we were going to sell her car and house. He immediately asked why upset her, which meant why tell her? True, we all wish to be honest and keep things above board. But there are times when it is best to say nothing. I could tell by his reaction that he had discussed this concern with others many times before. This conversation was very helpful to me.

As POA, I received some of her mail. One of these letters was from her medical complex, reminding her that she was due for a mammogram. Knowing this was important, especially since she was a breast cancer survivor, I contacted the nursing home to see if they could make the arrangements and transport her to the place for her mammogram. They said yes and did so. The mammogram exam turned out well.

Paying Edna's bills was not being done in an orderly manner throughout this entire process. Some of the bills I had Edna pay when I was with her before being admitted to the nursing home. Others I paid myself, such as utility bills, doctor bills, medicine, exterminator, lawn work, dog removal, etc. This amounted to over $1,700. The trust representative at the bank said they would reimburse me from Edna's assets if I could provide them an itemized list and copies of the bills, which I did and received payment. The bill paying now was pretty well on track with the bank as successor trustee of Edna's trust paying the bills.

The nursing home made periodic contact with the family of patients to go over their plan and status of their well-being. I was the one contacted for Edna. On a telephone call in June, I asked to have the beautician work with Edna and see that her fingernails were manicured and the podiatrist work on her toenails. I told them to use the funds in Edna's resident account to pay for this service, which they did, and to let me know when her resident account was getting low. They agreed.

Rose and some of the neighbors visited Edna occasionally. Rose would give us feedback on their visits. Edna always told them and anyone else that would visit her that she would be going home tomorrow or in a couple of days. Rose also mentioned that she and Edna had long-term care (LTC) insurance that was obtained through the bank. This was great news and the first that we had heard of it. Rose thought Edna had told us. Our attorney found the company, policy number, and procedure for applying. I called the company and was informed that, when approved, they would pay within a few dollars Edna's daily rate. This would continue for five years. The paralegal started to complete the forms for the LTC insurance application.

The bank as successor trustee of Edna's trust and I as POA on her behalf had to stay in close contact to make sure we were in sync. We had a teleconference to discuss Edna's nursing home account, income tax filing, LTC insurance, bill paying, finance status reporting, her house and car, personal property disposal, and income tracking. This was a very successful teleconference.

Now that the bank was working closely with me, I was able to get a handle on the content of Edna's trust. The assets that were in the trust that were not in the bank were transferred to the bank. Now everything except the life insurance policies with Prudential was in the bank, which made it more manageable. Edna's wealth was now around $1.6 million, not including her house. Again, how in the world did a secretary and a firefighter accumulate such wealth? The only answer is that they lived a simple life, made a few profitable investments, and saved for over forty years.

I was not the only one with health problems. Bessie was having problems with her tear ducts. After various attempts for corrective action, the doctors recommended surgery. This was done in May 2015. After a few months of follow-up reviews, her tear ducts were much improved.

It had been about four months since I had visited Edna. I was pretty well recovered from my surgery and thought it would be good to visit her. Bessie was also recuperating well from her tear duct surgery. I ask Mary to join us, and she agreed. The trust representative from the bank also agreed to join us. So I once again made reservations at the Comfort Inn in Collinsville, Illinois.

Chapter 6

FOURTH VISIT
7/19/2015–7/30/2015

Bessie had an eye doctor appointment the morning of July 19. We left for Saint Louis immediately following her appointment and stayed overnight at Winchester, Kentucky. The next morning, we proceeded on to Collinsville, Illinois. The folks at the Comfort Inn again were happy to see us.

The next morning, we left for the nursing home. The plan was to meet with Edna in the morning and then go to Edna's house to search for valuables and remove a few items that Mary and I wanted as heirlooms and keepsakes. Also, I wanted to make sure that there weren't any guns in the house. The reason for this concern was because Kim had found shotgun shells and .22 caliber ammunition during his and our attorney's earlier visit. Kim had gotten rid of the ammunition. But if there was ammunition, there was a good possibility of guns, and these I planned on turning over or at least reporting to the authorities.

Edna looked good physically and greeted us very warmly. Of course she said that she would be going home tomorrow or in a couple of days. I knew Edna liked to read, so I asked if she had access to the library, and she said yes. I told her that I would bring her some books the next day. I also asked if she had had an eye exam recently, and she said no. Mary arrived shortly after us. Robbin, Mary's daughter-in-law, drove her from Prairie Du Rocher, Illinois. Mary looked good and was in good spirits. Shortly afterward, the representative from the bank arrived. The nursing home staff was very cordial to us. The Hope ward was tightly controlled. It was easy to enter, but no one could leave without a staff member opening the door. This was how it had to be with dementia patients.

We needed to clarify some financial concerns with the nursing home. We met with the billing department representative and clarified how the billing should proceed, whereby the nursing home monthly bill should go to the representative at the bank with a copy to me. Any medical bills from doctors, prescriptions, etc. should go to the bank for payment. The personal needs for Edna, such as outings, beautician, etc., should come out of Edna's resident nursing home account. When her account needed replenishing, I should be notified, and in turn

I would notify the bank to send additional funds. This was a very worthwhile meeting.

Our next meeting was with the social worker. In general, everything was going well with Edna from his perspective. I asked him about getting an eye exam for Edna. She had said that she wanted her own eye doctor to do it. He knew of Edna's eye doctor and said that he would make the necessary arrangements to transport Edna to her doctor's office.

After an additional hour or so visiting with Edna, we went to lunch without her, which was how it had to be. We could not take her out of the nursing home for fear she would want to go to her house and see the dogs. After lunch, we met the bank representatives at Edna's house to look for valuables and to remove any items that Mary and I wanted. I couldn't find any guns. Hopefully, Les had gotten rid of them before his confinement to a hospital. The bank representative documented everything that was removed. Bessie and I removed her collection of figurines. I thought the figurines would be good for our girls as a remembrance of their aunt Edna.

The real estate representative from the bank was also there to assess what needed to be done to get the house on the market. This was a tall order because of all of the junk and personal property that had to be removed from the house and garage, plus all the refurbishment. The carpets were removed, but the odor from the dogs remained, which had to be dealt with.

The next morning, Bessie and I took some books to Edna, who was happy to receive them. We then went to the bank in Clayton, Missouri, for our meeting. All of the principal people from the bank were there in addition to our attorney. The bank representative for Edna's trust chaired the meeting, which was well organized. Prior to the meeting, she laid out all the items she had received from our attorney. She wanted Bessie and me to take whatever items we wanted. We took the coins, jewelry, and documents that were removed from Edna's safe, and the representative documented the items we took on her inventory sheet. All the bank representatives knew Edna, which made the meeting more personal.

We first discussed the bills and deposits, which seemed to be under control, especially after our meeting with the nursing home billing representative the previous day. The bank provided a briefing on how they manage money for investors. It seemed to me quite remarkable that the people from the bank knew Edna and spoke so highly of her. The representative for Edna's trust had me sign the required paperwork for the IRA new account necessary in managing Edna's assets. The real estate representative led the discussion on Edna's real estate, which amounted to getting an appraisal and a realtor fair market analysis once the house was cleaned out and refurbished. Then the house would be put on the market. Our attorney led the discussion on the handyman fraudulent-check activity. She had discussed this with one of her distinguished legal contacts and was told that we would not win in court because Edna would not agree to prosecute even though she was in a nursing home with dementia. We would spend a lot of money on legal fees and not win. Plus, we would never recoup the money because the money the defendant fraudulently obtained wouldn't be available. So we reconciled ourselves to not prosecute, which was painful. The meeting was very successful.

Bessie and I went to see the paralegal to sign papers to get a duplicate title for Edna's car because we couldn't find the original. I had recommended to the bank representative that we give Edna's car to Mary, and she agreed. We then spent a few days with family members before leaving for home.

Once home, I had a little time to go through the documents from Edna's safe. Low and behold, I found the original title to Edna's car. I then forwarded it to the paralegal, who was processing the transfer. Also, I found another life insurance policy from Prudential. I contacted Prudential for the current dollar value of both policies. Combined they were around $15,000.

Edna had a mini SUV 2008 Mercury Mariner. I thought it would be proper that Mary be given the vehicle. This would be in keeping with Edna's will, where all personal property, including vehicles, would go to Mary. I thought this might be difficult since the bank was the successor trustee. I earlier approached the bank representative, who was my main contact on the trust, and she agreed with my request. I had a copy of the title, so I signed it as seller on Edna's behalf as POA, had it notarized, and Mary signed as buyer. We had to do it this way for the DMV even though we included the gift form. The paralegal from the law firm handled this for us.

Edna's birthday was September 12. The nursing home sent me an invitation for a luncheon they were having for residents with a birthday in September. I couldn't attend, but I asked Mary to attend, and she did. I sent Edna a dozen roses to arrive on her birthday. Mary reported back to me that the gathering was very nice. She asked Edna who had sent her the pretty flowers, and she said Les. Also, when they were having the luncheon, Edna thought she was on the fourteenth floor of the bank building in downtown Saint Louis, where she had worked.

The application for long-term care insurance was submitted to the carrier. They needed additional information for approval, which was provided. I requested that they forward the monthly annuity to the nursing home and the back payments to the bank for deposit in Edna's account. The back payment was for the time between the day of admittance to the nursing home and the day of approval of the claim minus the first ninety days. I forwarded an e-mail to this effect to the carrier, as requested.

Everything seemed to be under control with Edna. She was receiving professional care and was in an improved environment and way of life. Her revocable trust was being managed properly with the bank as the successor trustee and me as the POA. Her 2014 income tax return was submitted in time in accordance with the extension. Her house was being refurbished for resale. Her car was in the process of being transferred to Mary. Her dogs had been moved to animal control for adoption. No more should we hear "I will do it tomorrow" from Edna. Knowing this, we were planning another visit to have a real visit with her without being faced with uncomfortable decisions to make. I made reservations at the Comfort Inn in Collinsville for November 11 to November 17.

Chapter 7

FIFTH VISIT
11/10/2015–11/18/2015

Bessie and I left home early in the morning on November 10. We stayed overnight in Winchester, Kentucky, and proceeded on the next day to Collinsville, Illinois. The folks at the Comfort Inn gave us the normal warm welcome. I was going to e-mail the nursing home and inform them of our planned visit. Bessie advised against this and suggested we make a surprised visit to see how things really were at the nursing home and confirm the good feelings we had with the conditions.

We visited Edna the next day. She was happy to see us and looked well physically. You really couldn't tell that anything was wrong with her the way she could carry on with a conversation, until she started repeating herself. I presented Edna with a mystery book knowing how she liked to read them. As usual, she said that she was in the nursing home only for a couple of weeks and would be going home tomorrow or in a couple of days. The conditions at the nursing home were great and confirmed our earlier positive feelings. Edna said that the food was great. Mary and Robbin arrived shortly after we did, which made Edna happy.

I had a series of subjects that I needed to address with the head nurse of the Hope wing. First, how was Edna's behavior? She said that Edna had no more wanting-to-go-home episodes, which was good news. The plan that we had agreed on to correct this problem was evidently working. Her overall behavior was great. She seemed to be more interactive with the other residents. Secondly, was she going to the beautician regularly? The nurse indicated that she was and was scheduled to go again that afternoon. Also, she was receiving a manicure regularly and seeing the podiatrist regularly. Thirdly, when was her last physical exam to include a blood test? She checked her computer and said it was in May, which was good news, and she was in good physical condition for her age of eighty years. Fourthly, when was her last psychiatrist exam? She said the day before, which was good news. I asked her if she thought Edna could resume going on outings. She suggested not for a while. This concluded my visit with the nurse, which went extremely well.

The next item on my list was to visit the social worker as a courtesy and to follow up on the eye exam that he agreed to schedule at our previous meeting. Unfortunately, the eye exam appointment was not scheduled. Edna wanted her own eye doctor to do it. He called the doctor's office and scheduled the appointment for November 19. I agreed that we pay the co-pay and for a person to accompany Edna during the visit. Patients with dementia cannot go outside the facility unattended. The co-pay and accompanying attendant were to be taken from Edna's resident account. Also, Edna's glasses needed repair (a screw was missing), which was going to be fixed.

The final item on my list was to visit the representative in billing. The purpose was to apprise her of the LTC insurance status with the carrier, which was in the final approval process. Once approved, the monthly annuity would be directly forwarded to the nursing home. Also, I wanted to make sure that they knew to contact the bank when Edna's resident account needed replenishing.

We then said our good-byes to Edna and went to a late lunch. Before lunch, Mary provided me with the four Norman Rockwell plates she had removed from Edna's house on my behalf. After lunch, Bessie and I went back to the motel and critiqued our accomplishments for the day and prepared for the next day review of preparing Edna's house for sale.

We met at Edna's house the next day along with both bank representatives for real estate and Edna's trust. All of the items from the house and garage had been removed. The workers were doing the refurbishing. The dog urine odor had subsided quite a bit with hopes that it would be completely removed when the hardwood floors were sanded and refinished. When the refurbishing was completed, the property would be appraised and a fair market analysis would be performed by a realtor. This would determine the listing price for the property. The property would then be put on the market for sale. Edna's car was still in the yard. Mary hadn't removed the car because the title transfer hadn't been completed in Jefferson City, Missouri, due to the backlog of work. Mary had told me earlier that they planned on putting the car on a truck and transporting it to the repair shop in Prairie Du Rocher, Illinois. I mentioned this to the bank representative, who told me to have Mary do this as soon as she could. The title work could catch up later.

Bessie and I then went to the nursing home to visit Edna. When we arrived, the billing representative happened to meet us in the lobby. She beckoned us to come into the social worker's office. This made us a little apprehensive for fear that something was wrong with Edna. The billing representative told us that after her beauty shop appointment the day before, Edna wanted to go home and started packing her things. She was able to quiet her down after talking to her for some time. The billing representative and social worker both thought it was due to so much activity with our visit and the beauty shop appointment that she was overwhelmed. They both said that if it occurred again, they would let me know immediately. The billing representative had sort of taken Edna under her wing, so to speak, which we certainly appreciated. We then went to Edna's room to visit. This was a surprise to her because she didn't expect to see us. We admired her hair, which pleased her. She didn't show any signs of traumatic behavior from the previous day. Bessie and I then went to Bessie's sister Wilma's house in Sparta, Illinois, for a visit before leaving for home in Maryland.

When we returned home, I called the nursing home billing representative to see how Edna was behaving. She told me that everything was well with Edna, which relieved much of my concern.

I then called the LTC insurance carrier for the status of Edna's insurance. They told me that it should be approved within a week or so. They would hold back ninety days from the date of admittance to the nursing home. I advised them earlier to start payments to the nursing home from the date of approval and all back payments to forward to me in the form of a check payable to Edna and me. As POA, I would see that it got deposited into Edna's account at the bank. The check was the bank's idea because the LTC insurance carrier wouldn't do a direct deposit to the bank for security concerns.

Edna had her eye exam on November 19 and was diagnosed as needing cataract surgery in her left eye.

She had had the surgery several years earlier in her right eye. This surgery was scheduled for December 8, and would be performed at a cataract center where Edna's eye doctor practiced. I checked with the head nurse in Edna's Hope wing to make sure that Edna would receive the proper pre-op and post-op care. Having gone through this myself, I knew that a strict eye-drop routine was required both prior to and after the surgery. I was assured that all these precautions would be taken by the nursing home. I was happy that I had raised the issue of Edna needing an eye exam earlier. The surgery was successful, and the nursing home did a good job in seeing that Edna was taken care of and that she was transported to the doctor's office as needed.

The LTC insurance carrier called to tell me that Edna's insurance claim had been approved. This was great news. They held back ninety days from the date of admittance, which was February 26, 2015, and would send me a check for May 27, 2015, through August 2015, which amounted to $20,800. The bank faxed copies of the September, October, and November bills they had previously paid to the LTC insurance carrier, as requested. The LTC insurance carrier said they never received them, so the bank agreed to resend them. One week later, the LTC insurance carrier sent me another check for $19,800 for September, October, and November, which brought us up to date on the back pay. This money was deposited into Edna's account at the bank. The LTC insurance carrier would not honor any prepayment bills. The bill to the LTC insurance carrier had to be for services rendered during that month and certified that the patient was still in the facility during that billing period. Up to this point, the nursing home had submitted bills for prepayment normally about two weeks early. I again told the LTC insurance carrier that I would like to see a streamlined procedure for payment whereby the nursing home would submit the bill directly to the LTC insurance carrier for the amount the policy authorized and the difference submitted directly to the bank for payment with copies sent to me. I really saw no point in my being in the loop for payment unless there was a problem requiring my assistance as POA. The LTC insurance carrier would work out the details with the nursing home and the bank. These are the kind of frustrating details you can face as POA. The LTC insurance was extremely important in that it paid within a few dollars the daily cost at the nursing home. This was to last for five years. The LTC insurance, coupled with profits from her investments, monthly income, and current wealth, should have more than covered her stay at the nursing home for many years. I was almost sure that we would never have to resort to Medicaid in the future for Edna.

The transfer of the SUV title from Edna to Mary was taking an extraordinarily long time. The paralegal at the law firm said that they always had better success dealing with Jefferson City, Missouri, than the local DMV. Mary had the vehicle moved by truck to an automotive repair shop in Ruma, Illinois. The paralegal finally called me, saying that she had received the paperwork from Jefferson City and was mailing it to Mary. Another mission was accomplished, assuming that Mary didn't have problems at the Waterloo, Illinois, DMV in trying to register the vehicle. I eventually received word from Mary that the title work had been completed as well as the mechanical work. Another mission was accomplished.

Bessie suggested that we send a sweater to Edna as a Christmas gift, which I thought was an excellent idea. I also thought it would be nice to send a sweater to the nursing home billing representative in appreciation for looking out for Edna. This was accomplished.

I received an invitation from the nursing home to attend a Christmas luncheon for the residents. Bessie and I could not attend, so I asked Mary to attend. She agreed and had Robbin drive her there. Also, I asked Mary to see if Edna had received the sweater. In an earlier conversation with the billing representative, she had indicated that she had received hers. I received feedback from Mary that the luncheon was great, and that Edna looked good physically and was in good humor. Mary asked her about the sweater I had sent her, and Edna indicated that she hadn't received it. During the luncheon, Edna again thought she was on the fourteenth floor at a bank building in downtown Saint Louis.

Everything now with Edna seemed to be under control. The legal matters were in the hands of a good attorney. The financial matters were in good hands with the bank as successor trustee of Edna's revocable trust. Edna's will and my being POA were under control. Edna's dogs had been put in the hands of the proper authority. Edna had received the proper diagnosis and was admitted to a great nursing home where she was receiving excellent care. She received her medications as prescribed, her food was excellent and nutritious, she visited the beauty shop on a regular basis, she got a manicure and visited the podiatrist on a regular basis, and her physical, psychiatric, and eye exams were done on a regular basis. Her car was given to our sister Mary, and her house prepared for the market. We didn't anticipate any urgent visits to Saint Louis. However, we did plan on visiting Edna at least quarterly. Mary would also visit Edna on a regular basis.

EPILOGUE

Sometimes things in life occur in mysterious ways. This certainly was the case in my experience with Edna. I often asked myself a series of "what if" questions concerning her. What if Edna had paid her telephone bill? I would have never heard the message, "The number you have called is temporarily disconnected." I therefore would have not requested assistance from organizations for the aging in Saint Louis, and who knows what could have happened, especially with Edna driving? What if I would have ignored the recommendation to call the representative on the hotline? I would not have received the professional services of the state representative supervisor and his staff, which really was the force in obtaining the corrective care for Edna. These are just a few "what ifs" to give you an idea of what could have happened.

The past year or so has been a very traumatic but overall a grateful time in Bessie's and my life.

Traumatic times in that we were faced with many situations that were unexpected and foreign to our lifestyle. Grateful times in that we were able to face situations and make decisions to improve the way of life for our loved one, Edna. The lessons we learned through this experience will hopefully benefit others.

One basic item I feel many of us are guilty of is not informing our loved ones, whether our children, siblings, distant relatives, or close friends, about our private matters. I realize that this is a very confidential part of our lives, but having someone knowledgeable in matters dealing with our financial accounts, will, funeral arrangements, etc. simplifies matters when we become incapacitated or die. In the case of Edna, no one knew much about her private affairs. We had to search through stacks of disorganized papers and make phone calls to financial institutions, former employers, insurance companies, and neighbors. All these efforts were conducted, not knowing if our search was complete. In our case, we had a State of Missouri representative prodding us for information and informing us of consequences, which forced us to act. Fortunately, Edna had more than average financial resources, which provided us the necessary legal and management assistance that we needed. I realize that many people faced with these situations won't have similar finances to work with, which presents a monumental problem when forced to rely on government social work organizations, Medicaid, etc. But on the other hand, we have to be thankful that we have these organizations and programs available to help.

Another important lesson that we learned was to pay closer attention to abnormalities in the behavior of our loved ones and the need to address the abnormal behavior right away. In our case, we didn't. We knew but ignored the first two signs, and it took the State of Missouri representative to get involved on the third sign. I often wonder what would have happened to Edna if I hadn't made that hotline call. It may not be easy to address a behavior abnormality with a loved one, but don't ignore it. There should be some way to diplomatically approach the condition. Doing this may prevent a catastrophe and enable your loved one to obtain needed medical help sooner. I often think how fortunate we were with Edna driving. She could have killed herself or some innocent person(s). If this would have happened, I would have felt at least partly responsible for not addressing my first observation of Edna.

There are those situations where the person needing assistance doesn't have caring relatives or friends to take the lead on his or her behalf in seeking medical care and management of his or her resources. These are not only destitute people but also the well-to-do, in many cases. Fortunately, in this country we do have government organizations to fall back on. Unfortunately, the average citizen is unaware of whom to contact in government when confronted with a situation of this type. My only suggestion is to contact any county or state official and explain the situation. They can steer you in the right direction to start the remedial process. Some of us are reluctant to contact government officials due to some unknown fear. Don't let that fear detour you from seeking help. Government officials, especially the elected ones, want to help their constituents and thereby gain your support in future elections.

Another unfortunate situation you may confront in trying to obtain help for a loved one suffering from a mental affliction is the myth and misunderstanding of mental illness. We sometimes fall into the trap of thinking, like we used to in years past, that anyone with mental illness should be admitted to nuthouse or crazy house with padded cells. Don't let this kind of thinking get the best of you. There has been much improvement made over the years in mental illness diagnosis and care. True, there is still much to be done, and progress is being made. Sometimes the main problem in seeking professional help is with the patient. "No, I am *not* going see a crazy or quack doctor!" is the response you can get from the one needing help. I probably would have been faced with this situation with Edna hadn't it been for the State of Missouri giving me no choice. I can only surmise how I may have handled it if they had never prodded me. I probably would have discussed the situation with a psychiatrist and proceeded with his or her recommendations. If that didn't work, I may have lied to Edna and told her that we had an appointment with a general practitioner and then escort her to the psychiatrist and go from there. You do what you have to do if you truly care for the person needing help.

I am very happy that we did what we did on Edna's behalf. After all is said and done, you really get a feeling of satisfaction in helping a loved one. I sincerely hope that our experience with Edna will help you in facing a similar situation.

Andrew J. Rickert has made his way amid the tumult of his sister's affliction with dementia. He decided to capture his experiences in writing and to share them with others who face similar circumstances in their own lives. He lives in Mechanicsville, Maryland.

Printed in the United States
By Bookmasters